GW00390861

Tortoises and how to keep them

Tortoises and how to keep them

MAXWELL KNIGHT, O.B.E., F.L.S.

*Revised edition brought up to date
and edited, including a new chapter
on* TERRAPINS, *by David Ball,
Overseer of Reptiles at London Zoo*

Illustrated by John Norris Wood

 BROCKHAMPTON PRESS

By the same author in this series
REPTILES IN BRITAIN

ISBN 0 340 03914 0

First edition 1964
Revised edition 1970   Second impression 1973
Published by Brockhampton Press Ltd, Salisbury Road, Leicester
Printed in Great Britain by Hazell Watson & Viney Ltd,
Aylesbury, Bucks.
Text copyright © 1964, 1970 Maxwell Knight
Illustrations copyright © 1964, 1970 Brockhampton Press Ltd

Contents

Readers may be interested to know that in 1966 *The International Turtle and Tortoise Society Inc*. was formed. Their address is : 8847 De Haviland Avenue, Los Angeles, California 90045, USA. PO Box 45555. They publish a journal every two months, full of useful information about turtles, terrapins and tortoises. Contributors include scientists, zoo personnel, vets and pet owners. Information ranges from involved scientific study to useful hints on feeding, housing, ailments and breeding.

1 What is a Tortoise?

This may seem to be a very easy question to answer because most of you will have seen a tortoise, while many of you may own one or want to own one. However, it is not at all uncommon for me to get a letter asking if a tortoise is a mammal. And I well remember one boy who stated proudly that a tortoise is an insect!

Tortoises and turtles and terrapins belong to the large class of animals called the *Reptilia* (Reptiles), which also contains the snakes, crocodiles, alligators and lizards. All the Reptiles have scaly coverings to their bodies; but tortoises and their relations are distinctive in also having shells into which they can withdraw in order to escape from enemies or from unsuitable weather conditions; and also to sleep, and when they hibernate.

It is often thought that the shell is an external skeleton such as insects possess – perhaps that is why my young friend thought a tortoise was an insect. The shell is not a skeleton of any kind; and all the many species of land and water tortoises have perfectly good internal skeletons which support or protect their limbs and internal organs.

These curious shelled reptiles have an ancient history which goes back some *two hundred million years*! They together with the crocodiles and alligators and one very primitive species of reptile (the Tuatara) from New Zealand, probably resemble their remote ancestors more than any other animals alive today. Those scientists who study the history and evolution of living things consider that this order within the class *Reptilia* has very likely passed its peak and is now on the decline. We need not concern ourselves with this in any detail, since such changes as may take place in the future will be spread over very lengthy periods – all the same it is interesting to know that the common species dealt with in this book had their ancestors living such an enormously long time ago.

There are about 237 species and possibly another 100 subspecies or races of tortoises, turtles, and terrapins in the world today, and these vary much in size. The huge Leatherback Turtle may weigh nearly 1,500 pounds and measure nine feet; the Giant Tortoises from the Galapagos Islands have been recorded as reaching a weight of over 550 pounds. The Old World tortoises have among them some very large species, and these are found on the islands of Aldabra and the Seychelles in the Indian Ocean.

At the other extremes are some land tortoises and also aquatic ones which are measured in inches rather than feet.

In Britain the name *turtle* normally refers to the marine species that live in the sea. *Terrapins* live in water, and nearly always fresh water. *Tortoises* normally live on land.

But these names have different meanings in the USA, and if you are talking to an American, you may find that he will use the word *turtle* to cover all these three different kinds.

As to distribution, we can say that the many species of these shelled reptiles are, according to their needs and habitats, found in widely separated parts of the world. Few are found in countries where the temperature is only moderate in summer: most come from tropical or subtropical regions, although a few species exist as far north as Canada. Curiously enough, there are no *land tortoises* in Australia, though many species are well distributed in Africa, India, and other Asiatic countries, and in North and South America – to say nothing of several groups of tropical islands. There are even a few species in the warmer southern countries of Europe.

Tortoises, whether from the tropics or from temperate climates, require a similar diet, and this will assist us when discussing food. In other respects, however, treatment varies, and is more specialized, for instance, in the housing and heating of tropical species. This makes them more difficult and expensive to keep and so they are not recommended for people who only want a tortoise as a pet. Their requirements will be discussed under the appropriate sections. The three species of land tortoises which are most commonly on sale in pet shops are the Spur-thighed tortoise, *Testudo graeca*, imported from North Africa; Hermann's tortoise, *Testudo hermanni*, which is imported in smaller numbers than the Spur-

9

Spur-thighed tortoise

thighed tortoise and comes from Southern Europe; and the Horsfield's tortoise, *Testudo horsfieldi*, from Western Asia.

The three species can be identified quite easily. The Spur-thighed tortoise has, as its name implies, a horny 'spur' on the back of its thighs. The supracaudal shield is undivided and there is no 'spur' on the tail.

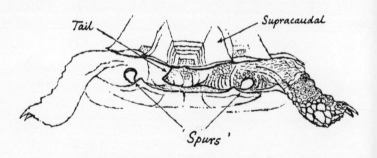

Spurs and tail of the spur-thighed tortoise
(the plate immediately above the tail is called supracaudal)

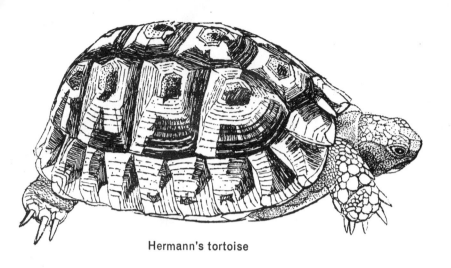

Hermann's tortoise

Hermann's tortoise does not have 'spurs' on the thighs, but it does have one on the tail. Also, the supracaudal shield is divided. Occasionally specimens are seen

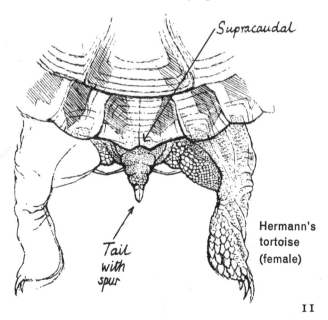

Supracaudal

Tail with spur

Hermann's tortoise (female)

that have features from both species; these are known as hybrids and occur where the ranges of the two species overlap.

Horsfield's tortoise is very easy to recognize as its shell is flatter than the preceding two and almost round. Also, it only has four claws on each foot. Both the other species have five claws on the forelimbs and four on the hind limbs.

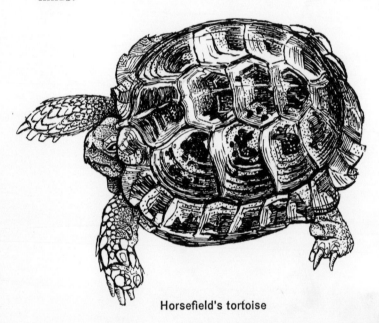

Horsefield's tortoise

The terrapins, being aquatic, will be discussed together with instructions on their care in captivity in a special chapter later on.

Now I want to tell you a little about how this book is set out so that you can use it to your best advantage. In the next chapter are some details about the general structure and the senses of tortoises. These matters are important because no one can keep an animal in captivity properly and wisely without some knowledge of its anatomy, senses, and general habits.

After this I shall deal with the equally important questions of when and where to buy a tortoise; how they are imported into Britain; the best way to house and keep them and, of course, to feed them. Some mention will be made about breeding because, though not all of you are likely to have a pair which will mate and lay eggs in Britain, this does sometimes happen. More often, a female tortoise which has mated before arriving here will lay eggs, and you will want to know the right way to deal with these should you be lucky enough to be faced with this task.

As to health and disease: this is really a matter for expert veterinary advice; but there are a few hints which I can give you about first aid that may save you grief and disappointment.

Leatherback turtle

2 Structure and Senses

The most obvious and remarkable feature of the land tortoise is of course the shell. This is made up of a series of hard horny shields which are arranged in a regular pattern. Those on the upper part of the shell, which is called the *carapace*, are in the form of a number of rings which themselves are dome-like and raised at the centre. The underpart of the shell, known as the *plastron*, is also composed of horny shields, but these are flattish. The particular way in which these shields are arranged is one of the means by which tortoises of various species can be identified. The shields are relatively thin and are attached

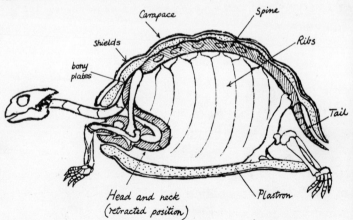

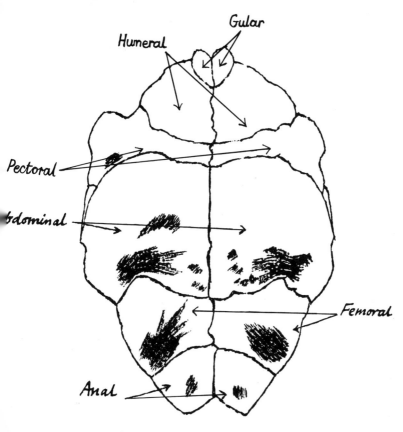

**Plastron of spur-thighed tortoise
showing arrangement of shields**

on their undersides to bony plates. The two, the shields
and the plates, make up the shell.

The upper and lower parts of the whole shell are joined
together, making a strong protective covering. In the front
of the shell is an opening sufficiently large for the tortoise,
when withdrawn into the shell, to have its head and its

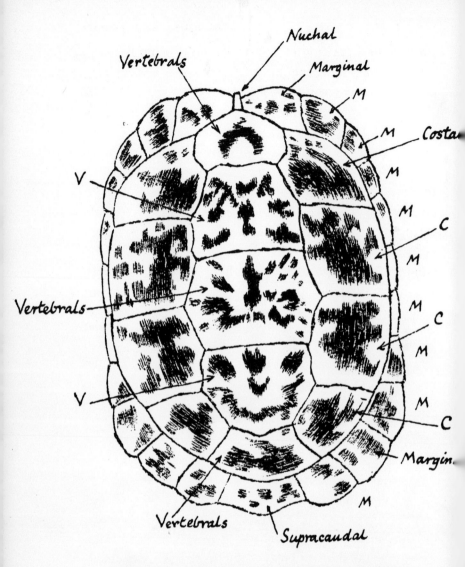

Carapace of spur-thighed tortoise showing arrangement
of shields: marginal = the edges of the shell; costals =
the region of the ribs; vertebral = the region of the back-
bone or spine; supracaudal = above the tail; nuchal =
the neck

forelegs in a position of safety, the head being between the two legs, with the latter placed across the opening and completely covering the head.

At the rear end of the shell there is another opening into which the hind legs can be withdrawn, the tail being bent to one side.

In addition to its other uses the underpart of the shell, the *plastron*, is one of the ways by which it is possible to find out if your own tortoise is a male or female. In male tortoises the *plastron* is concave or curved inwards towards the rear end, and in addition, the tail is longer and stouter than that of the female. The *plastron* in females is flat and the tail is shorter. The sexing of tortoises can only be reliably carried out with specimens over four

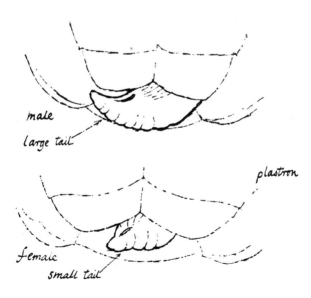

male
large tail

plastron

female
small tail

inches. This size indicates an age of about three or four years.

Many people think of the shell as being without life and without nerves and blood-vessels. This is not so. Within the inner parts of the shell are blood-vessels and nerves. It is important to know this because it is quite possible for the shell to be damaged and suffering caused to the tortoise if it is carelessly handled or knocked; during hibernation care must be taken that rats and mice cannot get at the resting tortoise and nibble the shell. The shell is, of course, very strong; but this does not mean that the tortoise likes being stood upon, nor that it can be dropped on to a hard surface without risk of harm!

THE HEAD AND LIMBS

The general shape of a tortoise's head is well known. The neck is quite long and is covered with soft skin; it can be thrust out or taken back into the shell with quite surprising speed if the tortoise is alarmed, though normally the head is pushed out slowly and deliberately.

Tortoises do not have teeth, but the jaws are covered by a hard and sharp ridge of horny material which is capable of biting through most vegetation which may be required as food. The grasping of leaves and stems is made easy by the fact that the jaws are almost beak-like in front, and this is most useful for getting at awkwardly placed stems of plants.

The eyes are at the sides of the head and are small and

very dark brown in colour. Eyelids are present and so is a so-called 'third eyelid'. This is a semi-transparent piece of skin that can be moved across the eye for protective purposes and is known as the nictitating membrane.

There are no external ears and the entrance to the inner ear is covered with a layer of skin called the tympanum.

The limbs of tortoises are worth some close study. The front limbs are covered with scales, and are flattish, with spade-like feet bearing five clawed toes with the exception, of course, of Horsfield's tortoise which has only four claws. They are well shaped for digging – a point that will be referred to again. The hind legs are not so scaly, being mostly covered with soft skin; the feet are

Spur-thighed tortoise

flattish beneath and stumpy. These back feet have often been said to have some resemblance to those of the elephant. There are only four claws on each hind foot.

THE SENSES

Though tortoises are probably short-sighted they can see well and can distinguish colours – yellows and reds seem to be the most attractive. Sight is used in finding and choosing food.

The sense of smell is excellent, and is used in conjunction with sight when feeding. Tortoises can certainly tell one green plant from another of the same colour by means of their powers of scent.

Whether tortoises can hear has been the subject of much argument in the past but it has now been established that they can receive airborne sounds. They are able to respond to other vibrations, especially from the ground. If the earth is stamped on or hit with a stick when you are out of range of a tortoise's sight, there will be an immediate withdrawal into the shell.

Tortoises can also make sounds as well as the usual hiss which is characteristic of reptiles. One of the South American tortoises and the Giant tortoises are capable of making grunts that can be heard many yards distance.

Tortoises, like snakes, lizards, crocodiles, and other reptiles, are cold-blooded. Put simply, this means that they have no regular body temperature of their own such as birds and mammals have. All reptiles respond only to the temperature around them. They are sluggish or even completely motionless in cold weather, and active when the weather is warm. They will not feed unless they have had time to 'warm up' and to keep warm, and a sudden drop in temperature will send them back into their shells until the temperature rises again. Even so, a really scorching hot day may be too much for them, and they will either seek a feeding place out of the direct sunlight, or they will get into a shady spot and remain inactive. I have found that in Britain a temperature of between $15.5°$ C ($60°$ F) and $26.7°$ C ($80°$ F) is suitable for tortoises. When it drops below $15.5°$ C ($60°$ F) they will begin to refuse food, and lower still they become torpid.

As to their intelligence, tortoises have small brains and cannot be described as being intelligent animals; but they are capable of recognizing their owners. This is probably due to the way in which a careful owner handles them in contrast to a clumsy or nervous touch by a stranger; or it may be due to their sense of smell. It should never be forgotten that to those animals with keen powers of scent we humans have our own kind of smell – however clean we are. Higher animals, such as dogs, can recognize each individual member of a family by his or her scent. It is not likely that tortoises can do this, but they are capable of knowing those who look after them and handle them regularly.

3 The Trade in Tortoises

This is a most important chapter because all the tortoises which we keep as pets come from other countries; and the way in which they are caught, packed, and shipped, and the way they are treated when they arrive in Britain, should be of concern to everybody. Things in this respect are much better than they used to be, but there is still room for improvement.

The vast majority of the tortoises which arrive in this country come originally from Morocco. Not so many years ago these unfortunate creatures were so carelessly collected, and so badly packed and crowded together, that not only did most of them suffer a great deal, but they actually died in great numbers. Thanks to the hard work done by the RSPCA and other interested societies, more attention was paid to the conditions under which tortoises were collected and shipped. One of the most important things which is now being done is to persuade the importers and the dealers in Britain, who buy the tortoises for resale, to limit the size below which it is undesirable for these to be caught and sent to this country. Any tortoise *less* than four inches in length is unsuitable, and unlikely to survive very long. Today there are far fewer of these 'baby' tortoises being offered for sale.

Numbers can be confusing if they are not clearly set out, but some idea of the quantities of tortoises that are imported can easily be understood when it is shown that recently something like one hundred and sixty thousand tortoises have been imported every year. If this kind of mass collection goes on it could mean that, before long, the population of tortoises in Morocco could fall to such an extent that the species will be in some danger.

I expect that many of you may think that such a huge figure means that more than enough tortoises would arrive in pet-shops to supply all those who wished to have one. But the saddest part of this story is that nothing like that number of tortoises even reach the shops. It has been shown that about one in ten of the tortoises which leave North Africa die before they get here! That is not all: many more die after arrival or are injured or damaged so much as to make them unsaleable.

So much concern was there about the plight of imported tortoises that some people who study reptiles, together with representatives of animal welfare societies, felt that steps should be taken to inquire into the possibility of having an Act of Parliament introduced which might limit the size of imported tortoises or even prohibit their entry in Britain at all.

There was much discussion about this; and one difficulty to be faced was whether a law banning the importation of tortoises with an under-shell of four inches or less could be satisfactorily worked. What eventually happened was the calling of a meeting of representatives of all persons and bodies concerned. This took place in February 1963 when the RSPCA, the British Herpetological Society, the Universities' Federation for Animal Welfare, and the dealers all sent one or more persons to put their points of view to the MP who would be presenting any Bill agreed upon.

There was a very free and helpful talk in which I, myself, was invited to take part. Shortly after this it was decided *not* to take any further steps towards a new law for one year. The dealers agreed to do all in their power to make it clear to the traders in North Africa that under-sized tortoises would not be acceptable for sale in this country.

Another important thing is that anyone who buys a tortoise should learn how it should be kept, housed, and fed before they buy it! If people are not prepared to go to some trouble over this then they should not have a tortoise – or, indeed, any other kind of pet.

If you take all reasonable steps to see that the tortoise you buy is healthy there is no reason why you should not have one as an interesting and long-lived pet. Tortoises are among the longest-living animals; and even the smaller species, with which we are dealing here, can easily survive for fifty years – and even more, but this is largely up to you. Tend your tortoise with care and it is possible that your children could enjoy the same one that you had when you were a child.

4 Buying a Tortoise

A large number of tortoises which are so eagerly bought each year by enthusiastic boys and girls die – often quite soon after purchase. This may be due to wrong feeding and treatment; but it is more likely to be because the young enthusiasts who buy them do not know how to select a good specimen when they are confronted with anything from a dozen to fifty, according to the size of the pet-shop.

The would-be tortoise keeper must take as much trouble over choosing a tortoise as would be taken over buying a dog. It is no use buying one just because of the colour of its shell; it is certainly not right to buy the smallest one in the shop; and it is always wise – when you have the choice – to be as careful in selecting the shop as you should be in selecting the tortoise itself.

Ask advice from your nearest zoo, or from the local RSPCA Inspector. If neither is possible, then consult someone you may know who has kept tortoises for some years or, perhaps, a naturalist who goes in for keeping pets of various kinds.

You may want to know how to tell whether a certain shop is good and reliable or not. I will give you a few hints on what to look out for. These do not mean that you must have a lot of knowledge; it is only necessary to read what I have to say and remember the points I make.

a) Go to the best shop you know of and bear in mind that the largest is not necessarily the safest.

b) When you go to the shop – together with a knowledgeable adult if you can – have a general look round the place first. The owners of such shops will not mind if you ask permission to do so. Do not immediately announce that you want to buy a tortoise; what you need is some idea as to how the other animals in the shop are caged and cared for. If the birds on sale, for instance, have clean cages and look in good plumage and, perhaps, can be seen feeding, then that is a helpful sign. If the shop has hamsters or fancy mice, look at these closely to see if there are too many in one cage or tank – these are often housed in old aquarium tanks because they are easier to display and can more easily be caught in such a container.

If the hamsters or mice are all huddled together and are seen to scratch a lot, or if the cage looks damp and dirty, you must beware. If the animals do not seem clean and lively you may be sure that tortoises will have had less attention than the birds and mice; for some dealers think that tortoises require little or no looking after, and this is quite untrue.

c) Having spied out the land, so to speak, you can then turn your attention to the tortoises. Have a general look at them first. You will usually find that they, too, are housed in tanks. If there are so many in one tank that they can hardly move about I would suggest you try another shop. You may find that they are housed out of doors in cold or damp weather without any shelter, or they might be left in the sun on a hot day without shelter. Again it is better not to buy these, but if they are kept in decent conditions and can move about and seem reasonably active, then the first test has been passed. See what food they have been given and whether this is fresh or whether it is stale and soiled. If the green-stuff passes your inspection, note if some of the tortoises are feeding (which they should be if the shop is properly heated) and mark these down as being worthy of further examination.

d) You can then ask if you may pick some up in order to have a closer look. If permission is refused – go elsewhere; but you will normally be allowed to handle them. Do this very carefully in case you drop one.

The first thing you want to know is whether the particular tortoise you pick up is quick in its reactions; therefore choose one that is feeding or one which at least has its head and legs protruding from its shell. If one of the hind limbs is held gently, the tortoise should try to pull its leg back into its shell. If it is fit, this will be done energetically.

Examine the shell with care and if it is soft, reject it and have a look at another. Check for any cracks or other damage. A tortoise with a cracked shell should never be bought, but a slight roughness at the edges need not put you off if the creature seems lively in itself. You will find that when you have had the tortoise in your warm hands for a few moments it may put out its head and limbs again. If this happens touch the head lightly but firmly with your finger; if the tortoise once again goes back into its shell this will confirm the similar behaviour you observed when first picking it up. So far so good.

Next you must have a look at its eyes and lips. These *should* be all right if the specimen you are looking at had been feeding when you first started your general inspection. The eyes should be bright, and if you gently touch them you may see the eyelids close before the tortoise pulls its head back. The jaws will probably be stained a little from the green food, but if there is any sign of a 'crust' where the jaws meet you should go on to examine another individual.

You cannot expect tortoises in a shop to have bright and polished shells and to be looking completely satisfactory in that respect; but there is a difference between a slightly dull shell and one which is definitely dirty. A good dealer should have given all his stock a wipe over with tepid water and also a drink when he first received them; there is no excuse for a shop tortoise being in a filthy condition.

e) Further points to look out for are the presence of 'ticks' clinging to the soft parts. Ticks are sucking parasites which look like greyish garden peas. The mouth parts are buried in the tortoise's skin and it is the stomach – probably full of blood from the tortoise – that looks like a pea. Should you find any ticks on an otherwise satisfactory specimen you need not refuse it on that account; but you will have to deal with these when you

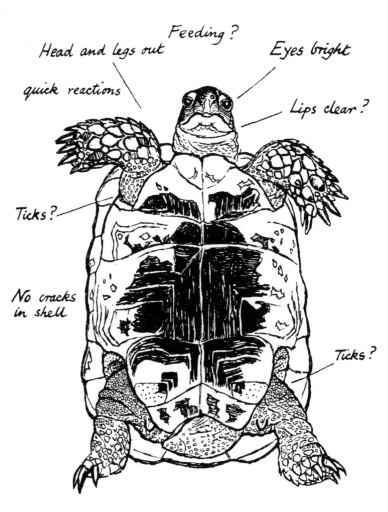

Feeding?

Head and legs out

quick reactions

Eyes bright

Lips clear?

Ticks?

No cracks
in shell

Ticks?

Should be good weight for size

POINTS TO LOOK FOR
(Spur-thighed tortoise)

Tortoise tick
(enlarged 5 times)

finally get your pet home. I shall tell you how to do this later on.

f) The last 'test' you should make is to try to obtain some idea of the weight of the tortoise which you fancy. This is not easy, but you can note its size and, if it feels light in comparison with its companions of the same length and bulk, it has either not been fed since its arrival or is going to be a difficult one to adapt to its new surroundings.

One final word about buying a tortoise: the time of year is most important. They are usually imported into this country from late March or early April and onwards through the summer. Therefore, do not buy one either too early or too late. May, I think, is a good month because earlier arrivals may not have fed before they were caught after coming out of hibernation in their native country, and they might have caught a chill coming over. Late buying is unwise since, if you get one in September, for instance, you cannot be certain that it has fed properly during the summer months and it will not have enough time to feed up under your care before it will be necessary for you to prepare it for its winter rest. A good four months of feeding in Britain is necessary if the risk of disappointment is to be avoided.

Keep these hints in mind, and do not consider them a waste of time. The effort is well worth while.

5 What do You do Next?

Having selected your tortoise, you will now be anxious to take it home, and it is wise to see that you have something suitable to carry it in. Do not just pick it up and carry it in your hands – you might drop it. A basket is best for transporting it, but a *strong* carrier-bag will do quite well.

When you reach home the first thing to do is to give it an opportunity to drink. Tortoises are thirsty creatures, particularly when they have been in a shop for some time.

You will have to provide a large pie-dish or a basin big enough to allow the tortoise to rest in it comfortably; the container must be absolutely clean, and should be filled with tepid – not hot – water (26.7° C; 80° F). The amount of water should be just enough to allow the tortoise to sit in it without covering its nostrils.

After a few moments the tortoise may push out its head and drink; this it does by opening its mouth and more or less gulping the water. Let it drink for as long as it wants. You may find that after you have put your pet into the water and it has begun to feel the mild warmth, it will be stimulated to eject from the underside of its tail some waste matter. Should this occur do not be alarmed, for this is a quite natural process. What you must do, however, is to see that it does not drink the dirty water.

As soon as it has got rid of the waste matter, take it out of the dish and empty the water away, refilling it as before with tepid water – it will then probably have a drink.

The tortoise should have his first bath and drink indoors unless the weather is very warm. If the sun is out and it is warm, let the tortoise roam about for a while; but you must keep your eyes on it in case it disappears into a flower bed without your realizing it. In spite of the old saying 'As slow as a tortoise', you will be surprised how quickly it can move and get lost if you leave it alone.

It may eat a little while wandering around if your lawn has any clover in it, or dandelion or plantain. Let it feed in comfort if it shows signs of doing so – it is a good thing if a newly bought tortoise settles down quickly. In the next chapter I shall deal with food and feeding, but before you think about this seriously, you have another job to do. You must tackle those *ticks* mentioned just now.

These will probably be attached to the soft parts, but I have found them between the scales of the legs. Before you start to treat these – or rather kill them – you must understand one thing about them. All you will probably see of the ticks is their full stomachs; the biting and grasping parts will be buried in the skin. You *must* get the whole of the tick out, not just the part you can see.

Never try to pull them off with tweezers – you will only detach the stomach, leaving the rest in the skin. This can lead to sores which will become troublesome and difficult to treat.

You must have at hand a feather or a small paint brush,

and either some ordinary liquid paraffin or some methy-lated spirit. A drop or two then placed as near as you can get to the head end of the tick will usually cause the para-site to loosen its hold. Then you may use the tweezers (which should not be pointed ones) gently to pull the tick away. Do not be in a hurry to do this; an extra drop of the liquid you use is better than failure to detach the complete tick. You can tell if you have been successful by examining your 'catch' closely – with a magnifying glass if neces-sary. You will be able to see the legs and mouth-parts if you have been successful. Continue with this treatment until you are sure that your tortoise is free from ticks. Dispose of the corpses by burning them.

Many people want to know if it is right to put some-thing on to the place where the tick has been in order to aid healing. My own view is that, if you have been careful in your operations, you need do no more than wipe the spot with a clean rag. If you have not been as careful as you should have been, and there is any obvious wound, you should dilute some Dettol to a weak solution and apply a drop or two of this to the affected place. Your vet would also provide you with an ointment or paste suitable for small wounds.

If you were careful in your original inspection of your tortoise you should not have much tick trouble. The hints I have just given you are just in case you overlooked one or two ticks in the first place.

6 Foods and Feeding

Tortoises are primarily herbivorous but they do require some protein in the form of animal matter. They will eat meat, fish, and even some invertebrates, such as insects and garden snails.

Before going on to list the plants which tortoises like. I want to say a little about quantity. In writing about pets in general I always warn readers not to overfeed birds, mammals, and fish; this is because such overfeeding leads to too much fat and to illness.

Tortoises seldom, if ever, overfeed. They will eat as much as they want in warm weather, and you need not worry about their taking in too much food. They are more often underfed than overfed. This is because if we have a cool summer there may be weeks on end when the weather is so bad – wet, or cold – that tortoises are not sufficiently warmed up to be able to feed. Should this happen it is wise to put the tortoise temporarily in a corner of a warm room, in a large box, and feed it there. It is necessary that, during the spring and summer, a tortoise should be able to put on enough fat to last it through the winter months when it should be hibernating; and it is most important that it should feed well towards the end of summer.

In respect of the *amount* of food that a tortoise requires, a single tortoise should eat a quantity of food *at least* equal to one whole lettuce per day. Lettuce is relished by tortoises, but it must be remembered that lettuce, as a plant, is made up largely of water and that it is less nourishing than – say – several dandelion plants or a good feed of clover.

Another feeding tip to bear in mind is that, in the wild, tortoises browse on the plants they eat – they pull the leaves from growing plants. In captivity also they will prefer to eat green-stuff that is growing, rather than a pile of leaves put down for them. You see, it is easier for the creatures to eat from a rooted plant – they can grasp the leaves firmly and bite them through.

This does not apply to a lettuce, which is quite large and from which they can pull off most of the leaves. I suppose an ideal way of feeding tortoises on lettuce would be to plant a row especially for them so that they could eat them when they are rooted; but this will not often be very easy to arrange. Such foods as tomato cut in two, or raspberries which have fallen from the canes, or nearly rotten apples will be eaten without much difficulty. Wild plants, and any garden greens that can be spared are best pulled up by the roots and fed to the tortoises *complete*; they can feed more easily if this is done as there is some weight to pull against.

A word or two about water. It is often said that as a tortoise gets water indirectly from the vegetation it eats, there is no need to have water supplied. This is quite wrong, particularly in dry weather; and a pie-dish of water should be sunk in the ground so that the tortoise can get its head into it. If the dish provided for water is deep it is advisable to place a few stones or a sloping shelf of wood in it to assist the tortoise in climbing in and out. The water level must be kept up, and the water must be clean. The level is important because a small tortoise seeking to drink from a dish with only a little water in the bottom may climb down into it and have some difficulty in getting out again. I remember hearing of a tortoise that drowned after lowering its head end into the water below it; in consequence, its tail end was tilted at such a steep angle that it could not struggle upright again. No one noticed what had happened until it was too late.

If, after careful observation, you do not see your tortoise drink, spray its vegetable food with water before feeding, and give it a warm bath once a week, not forgetting to keep it inside until dry if it is a cold day.

Giant tortoise

This may be an appropriate place to warn you against the danger which may arise if a tortoise – for one reason or another – topples over on its back. Unless its waving legs or head can get some purchase against a solid object it may well be impossible for it to get back on its feet again. A period of only a few minutes may not matter much, though the tortoise will not like it; but if the proper position cannot be regained and the tortoise is left upside down for, say, an afternoon, it *can* die. The weight of its internal organs pressing in the wrong direction will affect its breathing. Death can also occur if a tortoise is on his back while in direct sunlight on hot days.

Now back to food. It may be argued that lettuces are expensive to buy, and unless you grow them in some numbers in the garden it will not be easy to supply the one lettuce per day per tortoise that I referred to. This amount was only mentioned as a guide to quantity – not as a rule to be followed exactly. A tortoise fed only on lettuce will not be as healthy as one which has a variety of food-stuffs; this desire for variety applies also to many other animals kept as pets.

Another point to be remembered is that stale or partly rotting plants will not help a tortoise – in fact they may be ignored. I have heard so often that a friendly green-grocer has kindly but thoughtlessly offered some lettuces that are not fit for sale to the public. These will be limp or even beginning to decay. If you get such an offer you must inspect these lettuces to see if they have any fresh leaves at all; if there are some in the 'heart' of the lettuce they will do for a snack after you have pulled off the bad leaves. If, on the other hand, nearly all the leaves are soft and slimy, refuse the offer politely. It is fair to say that a lettuce, little of which you would eat yourself, is not good enough for a tortoise either.

Many of you may not live within easy reach of the country and may therefore have to rely on household vegetables and fruits. In addition to lettuce, cabbage, the large leaves of sprouts, kale, greens and other similar vegetables will be eaten. Tortoises will also eat root vegetables such as carrots, turnips and swedes. These will require grating before offering them as they are hard to bite through. They are also fond of leafy twigs, with leaves attached, from the suckers thrown up from fruit trees; but be careful to consult your parents before giving these – you will not be popular if you strip twigs or small branches from fruit trees which may in due course bear fruit! And remember that a tortoise let loose in a garden cannot be expected to know the plants you value from those which are less valuable. This applies particularly to flowers.

Tortoises love eating certain flowers such as pansies, sweet peas, snapdragons (antirrhinums), fuchsias, hibiscus, roses and many others. Then there are the rows of garden peas which you may have. A tortoise will make short work of these just when they are starting to climb up the sticks. It will bite through the stem and eat what it wants, ruining the plant in the process. Of course when peas have been picked, and if there are still fresh leaves on the stems these may, if it is possible to do so, be pulled up and the remnants of the plant be given to the tortoise which will browse on the now useless stems and leaves.

Do *not* give the leaves of rhubarb or spinach to tortoises, nor pea-pods. The first two are not suitable and may be poisonous to tortoises, while pea-pods are too stringy and tough.

Fruits of many kinds are much liked by tortoises, with sliced tomato high on the list. Ripe plums which may fall from a tree are a great treat and so are raspberries, strawberries, and peaches when in season. They will also enjoy apples, pears, oranges, grapes, melons, blackberries and cherries (do not forget to remove the stones first). The harder fruits will have to be shredded before offering them. A banana (skinned) will be greedily taken by some individual tortoises, but do not forget that even this humble reptile has its own fancies: one will eat banana or a fallen apple which may have been attacked by wasps, while another will not touch these fruits. Tastes differ in tortoises just as yours do. Remember also its fancies may vary from one month to the next or from one season to another, so, because it has refused a certain food in the past, it does not mean to say it will not accept it if offered at a later date.

If you ever have the luck to hatch out tortoise eggs bear in mind that the babies cannot deal with cabbage leaves or even whole lettuce leaves for some time. These tiny little creatures must be specially catered for and they will do well on thin slices of tomato and lettuce, as well as all

Hermann's tortoise

the other food mentioned, provided it is finely shredded.

Leaving the garden produce, we come to the many wild plants that tortoises eat. The following are best and safest: dandelion (flowers and leaves), plantains, yellow trefoil, vetches, clovers, groundsel, chickweed and, of course, grass. You should look these up further in your flower book.

I mentioned earlier that tortoises required protein; this may have come as a surprise to some of you but zoos and many tortoise owners have been providing their tortoises with proteins, carbohydrates, fats, extra vitamins and minerals for many years. These extras can be offered in a number of ways; one of these is to sprinkle various 'meals' (liver meal, bone meal, fish meal and mineral meal etc.) over their vegetables and fruit. Most of you, however, will find it easier to provide these important foods in a far simpler form. They will eat sprats, shrimps, small snails, insects, tinned cat and dog foods, boiled eggs, bread, minced beef, liver, cheese and even kitchen scraps such as cooked vegetables, meat and fruit, etc. Some tortoises are very fond of cereals such as Farex or Bemax mixed with sultanas, raisins and milk into a porridge. Of course you can mix a number of other fruits, shredded vegetables and even extra vitamins, though the two cereals mentioned do contain a very well-balanced vitamin and mineral mixture.

Other tortoises seem to prefer one or other of the cereals sprinkled over their greenery. If the lettuce or cabbage is washed under the tap, then shaken, they should be still damp enough for the cereals to adhere to them. All the foods that I have mentioned have been relished by different tortoises, so please remember that although the tortoise is primarily a vegetarian it does require other types of food as well. It has been taken from its natural home where it could wander and feed at will and brought to a much cooler climate, and it relies on YOU to provide the correct food, minerals and conditions if it is going to survive. A few Spur-thighed tortoises have been known to live over 60 years in this country. Some of them may have been exceptionally hardy ones but there could have been thousands more if only owners took their responsibilities seriously. Now I do not suppose for one minute all tortoises will like every one of the foods that have been mentioned but among the list there are bound to be a number that will be enjoyed. Also it is not necessary to offer these foods at every meal; four or five times a week would be quite sufficient.

You will have little need to hunt high and low for wild plants for your pets. The ones I have mentioned are common and, at all costs, do not try experiments with wild plants. It is true that most animals seem to know – by scent or instinct – which plants or other foods are distasteful or harmful, but accidents can happen and there is no sense at all in taking risks.

The various foods I have recommended will keep a tortoise in good health and will allow it to maintain its strength and to store up enough energy to last it through winter.

Here is an important point which relates to health and feeding, but of which many people are unaware. A tortoise may come across a piece of natural chalk, or an old bone left by a dog or even a partly charred bone which has been burnt in the domestic stove and then thrown away. To the surprise of the observer the tortoise will be seen to nibble at it – sometimes quite energetically. This is because tortoises can lack a chemical substance called *calcium*, which is found in chalk and bones. They instinctively eat anything which contains calcium if they can get at it.

A lack of calcium can lead to brittle bones and what is known as soft-shell. Newly bought tortoises which have not been fed, or which have been improperly fed, may have these conditions. It is quite easy to cope with this so long as the lack of calcium has not gone on for too long. The substance popularly known as *cuttle-fish-bone* and which can be bought at most pet-shops is good. It looks like a piece of flat white bone, hard and shiny on one side and softer on the other. It is usually sold to bird fanciers. Buy a few pieces of this substance and put them in your enclosure where the tortoises will, if they need it, nibble from time to time. Baby tortoises should have a little of it grated finely and scattered on their food. Adult tortoises will prefer the whole piece and unless one is sick, there is no need to grate and sprinkle it around. There are, of course, other products such as calcium powder and bone meal and other mineral mixtures which can be sprinkled on to the food, but proprietary dog and cat food contains calcium and other minerals. Tortoises will also obtain calcium from white bread, the bones of sprats, and even ground egg shells.

Finally, remember the main points I have made : give plenty of fresh food daily; give variety when you can; offer food twice a day if your pet does not have access to grass and other plants; and don't forget water. If you get a healthy tortoise to begin with and you feed it as described here, you should never have to call in a veterinary surgeon unless you have to deal with an accident – then, call him in at once. Never forget that temperature plays a vital part in the feeding of tortoises, but they don't like being baked for hours in really hot sun !

7 Where Should Your Tortoise Live?

There are almost as many different views about where to keep tortoises as there are chapters in this book. This can be most confusing to a beginner. In spite of the variety of opinions there are some rules that should be followed as closely as possible.

The first is that, unless you are prevented by your own housing circumstances, the correct place in which to keep your more hardy tortoise is out of doors and not in a room of any kind. Tortoises must have a considerable amount of sunlight and heat from April until October – if they do not get this they will not thrive well.

The second rule is that tortoises must have a box or other shelter into which they can retreat either from rain and cold, or from blazing sun hour after hour. Although sun is necessary for them to enjoy activity and to enable them to feed regularly, they will seek shade of some kind if they become too hot for too long a time.

The third point to remember is that in the countries where they normally live, they frequent sandy and rocky places — not soft and damp situations. Hard or gritty ground is good because it not only helps the tortoises to keep their claws from growing too long, but it also keeps its warmth and directs this upwards. Damp places and soft grass are less useful in this way. Of course tortoises will enjoy browsing on a lawn in good weather, and ambling about on it for a time. It would therefore be ideal if both types of terrain could be incorporated together with an area of natural shade such as that offered by a shrub.

In considering whether you should keep a tortoise as a pet you must think about where you can keep it before you buy it. If you live in a flat, then, in my opinion, a tortoise would be most unsuitable unless you are prepared for the expense of heating and lighting and, equally important, can provide a large enough area for their accommodation. On the other hand many town houses may have little or no garden, but they may have an outside yard; and if this gets the sun for some hours each day a tortoise will do well there.

A point that puzzles many people is whether they are to allow their tortoise to roam about a garden freely, or to keep it in some kind of enclosure. If the garden is escape-proof and does not contain any valuable plants by all means let your tortoise roam at will; the more space it has the better. You will soon learn its daily routine and be able to find it without too much trouble. If this is not possible, then I would advise you to make an enclosure. This will prevent it from getting lost, for tortoises are great wanderers. They are also fine diggers. And I have known many cases where a tortoise has just walked out of a gate on to a road and then has either been injured by traffic or has gone off – never to be seen again.

Before going on to discuss enclosures, I must deal with the horrible practice of 'tethering' tortoises by drilling a hole in the edge of the shell and threading a string through it, the other end of the string being fastened to a peg in the ground. This is objectionable from every point of view.

In the first place there is great risk of damaging the shell badly and, of course, hurting the tortoise. Then there is the fact that these creatures normally walk in a straight line ahead. If tethered, they will not, when they reach the farthest distance allowed by the string, turn and move in a circle. They will, more often than not, go on trying to continue on a straight course. This may well lead eventually to their falling over on their backs. There have been many cases of death occurring through this – particularly on really hot days. The string is also liable to become entwined around various objects which further restricts the tortoise's movements and, on occasions, they have become entangled with fatal results. Therefore, if you cannot offer your tortoise the freedom of the garden an enclosure of some kind is the best way of confining your tortoise.

The use of an enclosure does not mean that you should never let it have a walk on a lawn or garden path – this is good for it; but you should only do this when you have the time to keep an eye on your pet and prevent it from getting lost.

If you have more than one tortoise, you must clearly have a larger enclosure than you would require for one; but the area for one tortoise should not be less than 10 feet by 6 feet – more if you can spare it.

First of all the ground must be prepared. If there is any long grass, most of it should be cut short and the remainder dug up. There is no objection to leaving some grass, dandelion roots or clover for the tortoise to eat. The rest of the area may be dug over and some broken bricks and large stones put in. On top of this there should be a mixture of sand and soil with a large number of stones included. If it is possible for the enclosure to contain a shrub this will provide an area of shade and shelter from the direct rays of the sun without loss of light. This in turn will encourage the tortoise to feed, which it will not do in the darkness of its box.

The situation chosen should face south or south-west, if possible, as that will allow more sunlight. You will aid drainage by putting your enclosure on a slight slope and, if you can manage it, arrange to construct your enclosure against a brick wall or wooden fence, as this will save making four sides. If there is only a fence, you must see that the bottom of it is very well bordered with larger stones or broken brick in order to discourage digging underneath the fence. You must have a drinking place in the 'pen', and a pie-dish let into the earth so that its rim is at ground level will be quite satisfactory.

The sides of the enclosure could be made from wood but are best made from asbestos sheets; these are weather-proof and will last for years. These sheets need not be more than 12–18 inches in height – quite enough to prevent the tortoise climbing out. Fasten the sheets to wooden posts, 2 inches by 2 inches, and be careful to have the posts *outside* the enclosure, with the asbestos sheets nailed to it with special nails which have large heads to them and a fair-sized washer as well; this prevents cracking and makes the whole structure firmer. These nails can be bought from any good ironmonger.

It is as well to drill holes through the asbestos, just big enough to take the diameter of the nail. This will make sure that your sheets will not crack when you are fastening them to the posts.

I used to make my enclosures or pens with wire netting, but I have now given this up because I found that the tortoises were inclined to try to climb out *via* the netting, and at times they would catch their claws in it or tumble over on to their backs. I have never found this happening when asbestos sheets were used – they are too smooth to allow the tortoise to get any leverage on them. Nor does it seem to happen with plastic netting of a fine gauge, which one can buy nowadays, providing it slopes towards the centre of the enclosure.

The enclosure is now almost complete – and the only further thing required is a shelter into which the tortoises can retire when it is raining or when they are ready for sleep at night. A stout wooden box will do well for this, but you must see that it is tilted backwards a little so as to allow the rain to run off it. The top and sides of the box

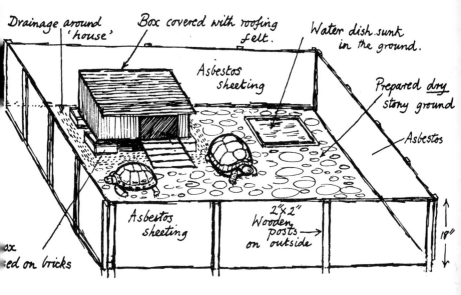

Drainage around 'house'

Box covered with roofing felt.

Water dish sunk in the ground.

Asbestos sheeting

Prepared dry stony ground

Asbestos

Asbestos sheeting

2"×2" Wooden posts → on outside

18"

...ox ...ed on bricks

must be covered with roofing felt nailed neatly down.

The box should be raised a little from the ground to keep it free from damp and this can easily be done with a few old tiles. If you place two layers of tiles along the underside of the open end of the box this will do admirably and also be a means of tilting the whole thing backwards.

Of course the tortoises will want to be able to climb into the box without difficulty, and so you should make a little ladder from the open front of the box down to the ground. This is best done by having a piece of wood about 18 inches long, across which you have nailed strips of wood to help the tortoise to walk up easily. The ladder need not be fastened permanently to the box; if it is just laid on the edge of it, the bottom end can be pushed into

49

the stones and earth that form the ground covering of the pen. The shelter should contain a few handfuls of hay into which the tortoise can burrow.

If you have the time and skill to make a more elaborate 'house', or if you are lucky enough to have a father or brother who is a good carpenter and who is willing to help you, then a specially built shelter will be better in every way.

Perhaps I should say here that whatever type of shelter you build, it will only be to provide a place which is free from damp, is screened from the direct rays of the sun, and is for the use of the tortoise in rainy or cool weather and for sleeping in. It is not for use during hibernation, which is dealt with in a later chapter.

If you are unable to build your enclosure on a slight incline the one thing you want to avoid is water collecting round the shelter. The rain will run off the roof and, unless you see that it can drain away quickly it will collect at the back and sides of the house. A good way of preventing this is to dig a little trench round the shelter – if possible a little deeper as it goes towards the back. This trench need only be from 4–6 inches deep.

Having dug the trench, put some rubble – broken tiles, bricks, or stones – in the bottom of it to a depth of 2–3 inches. Cover this with fine sand and you will have provided a kind of drain to soak up the water quickly. The water will go through the sand, which will dry out as soon as the rain stops. The water will continue to drain away through the rubble and will eventually sink into the earth. It is well worth taking the trouble to carry out this task. It does not take long to do.

I would like to say something about a more elaborate enclosure because up to now we have been discussing only the essentials required to confine tortoises. With a little thought and ingenuity the tortoise enclosure could enhance the appearance of the garden. It may be you have a neglected corner (facing south) or a flower bed where the plants have tough stems and the leaves are out of reach of the tortoises. Possibly part of the garden is terraced or perhaps you have a rockery that is not too steep that could be incorporated into an enclosure. Even if you have none of these features, a decorative enclosure could be built. First the ground. This needs to be on a slight incline for drainage and facing south. However, there is no need for it to be flat and uninteresting; a pile of earth, sand and rock here and there would add relief. A few rocks forming a cave could be built upon a rectangular polythene bin; this would make an ideal shelter. Before you start, remember to place the bin on four small supports so that it is raised off the ground. The open end of the bin could be partially covered so that the interior is not too exposed. Instead of a dish of water make a shallow pool, 2–3 inches deep in the centre, and, provided the sides slope gently to the centre and there are no steep edges, it will be a simple matter to brush the dirty water out of the pool. The wall of the enclosure would need to be 12 inches high and could be built in concrete with large stones and rock included if available. Alternatively, breeze blocks could be used and could be given a cement wash when in position. Finally, one or two shrubs and those flowers with tough stems could be planted; so also could some edible plants, though these would have to be protected until they were large enough to be eaten.

You may find that it is quite a good idea to have also a movable pen in which the tortoises can be put on your lawn in order to give them a change of diet – growing clover, for instance. This enclosure can be moved from place to place on a lawn on fine days so that the tortoise can have a fresh area in which to crop the clover and sun itself.

These pens are very easily made from the same materials as you used for your main enclosure – asbestos sheeting, wood or netting. A temporary shelter will be needed in case of rain or excess sun.

Every now and again we have summers with an exceptionally high rainfall. At these times, I feel extra shelter should be provided by a few feet of corrugated perspex placed across part of their enclosure. If you find your tortoise will not feed, however, I suggest you bring it indoors and keep it at a temperature of 21·2° C (70° F), or even a little higher until the weather turns warmer.

You must remember, of course, that tortoises have to get rid of waste-matter just as dogs and cats and rabbits do. This waste-matter, if left, attracts blow-flies, which is a most undesirable thing. The droppings should be removed at least three or four times a week and should be buried – not just thrown away anywhere.

I am aware that all I have written on the subject of 'housing' up to date has been aimed at those of you who have a garden of some kind. Does this mean that if you have no garden at all you must not keep a tortoise? I have mentioned that some town dwellers may have no garden, but they may have a large yard which is usually floored either with concrete or tiles. Such a place is quite satisfactory so long as it gets a reasonable amount of sun and has some kind of drain to run off rain-water. You must also have a shelter like the one I have described.

Such a yard – and the temporary pens referred to just now – must be kept clean. There must also be some means of supplying drinking water. In a temporary pen a deep saucer will do, but in a yard this is not so easy. You can, however, place a pie-dish in a shallow wooden box – a seed box will do. This box must, of course, be slightly bigger than the pie-dish. Fill the box with loose earth, then take out enough of the earth from the middle of the box and push the pie-dish into this hollow. The rim of the pie-dish will now be level with the earth and the top of the box, which should be pushed into the angle of a wall to keep it steady. Make a 'ladder' leading up to it and the tortoise will scent the water and be able to reach it easily. Alternatively, the dish could be set in concrete which could form a rim some four inches wide around it and the sides could slope gently to the ground.

How about those boys or girls who live in a flat? This is the most difficult tortoise-keeping problem of all. I dislike very much advising *against* keeping any kind of pet;

but it must be borne in mind that unless an animal can be provided with suitable surroundings and proper care, it is cruel to keep it in captivity.

In a flat or in a house with no garden it is almost impossible to maintain a tortoise in good health. Sunlight it *must* have – and where are you going to ensure that it will get it and, at the same time, allow it reasonably free movement? Unless you are fortunate and have a room given up completely to your pets you cannot make certain that a tortoise will have enough room or enough sun.

If your flat has a balcony your tortoises should be given every opportunity of fresh air and sunshine during the warmer months.

There may be other times when tortoises have to be housed indoors. I have already mentioned one, and that is during long spells of cold or wet weather. You may have a sick tortoise that is too weak to hibernate, or possibly you have hatched some tortoise eggs and have some babies. These, of course, should not be hibernated, as it is doubtful whether they would have enough time to build up stores of fat. It should be remembered that the cooler weather starts earlier in our climate and that our winters are more severe. Tortoises from the tropics should not be hibernated. They will remain awake throughout the winter and will require feeding. It is to be hoped that they spent some time outside during the summer on warm sunny days. It is not advisable to leave them outside at night unless the weather is exceptionally warm.

While tortoises are being housed indoors they will

require heating and light. During the summer months all that the tortoises will probably need, with the exception of those from the tropics, will be lamps suspended above them. If it is only one tortoise or two or three baby tortoises that are being housed in a cage or large box, one lamp will probably be enough. If you have a whole room set aside for a number of tortoises you are going to need more lamps.

If lamps are the only source of heating, this will mean that the tortoises would be under their glare for 24 hours a day. There are a number of ways of avoiding this situation. Their shelter could be made light proof by hanging curtaining material across the entrance. Alternatively, a blue or black night lamp could be used. This would produce some heat without the glare of light. Another method would be to heat the cage from underneath with an electric lamp fitted into a metal box or a biscuit tin.

The common tortoises (the Spur-thighed tortoise, Hermann's tortoise and Horsfield's tortoise) will feed at a temperature of 21·1° C (70° F) – 23·9° C (75° F). You will need a thermometer to measure the temperature in the cage. If the first attempt at getting the correct temperature fails, there are a number of ways of overcoming this. The light should be raised or lowered from its original position or if this is impossible, use a higher or lower wattage bulb. Another method of raising or lowering the temperature is to allow more or less ventilation. A night temperature of 15·6° C (60° F) – 18·3° C (65° F) would be sufficient.

Tropical tortoises should only be kept by those who have had experience with the more common species and have some knowledge of heating requirements. Up to now we have only been discussing heating by means of electric lights in the limited area of a cage. This may not be sufficient for tropical tortoises who require more space and a higher temperature which would be supplemented with electric heaters, oil stoves or radiators. These tortoises function best at a temperature between 23·9° C (75° F) – 29·4° C (85° F) during the day. At night there should be a drop of 5° C (10° F) when the lights are turned off. The cost of heating plus the price of food makes them rather expensive animals to keep.

Then there is the question of cleanliness. Tortoises can be messy creatures indoors; and even if one is kept in a special room you will have to cover the floor with some absorbent material although naturally it would be preferable if part of your floor could be covered in gravel, sand and stones. Newspapers will make a suitable floor covering for cages that are in temporary use.

I hope you will all see from this that, except under special circumstances, a tortoise should not be regarded as an indoor pet. To keep one in a kind of glorified rabbit hutch is most undesirable, though I am afraid that quite a few are kept like that.

8 Hibernation

This chapter is, perhaps, one of the most important in the book; and it is necessary first to understand something of what is meant by hibernation and what goes on inside an animal when it does hibernate.

The meaning of the word hibernation is 'resting during the winter'. It is often described as *winter sleep*, but this is not correct, for hibernation is not the same as sleep. When we, or other animals sleep, our breathing goes on in much the same way as when we are awake; food can be digested during sleep, and the circulation of the blood continues as usual. It is also quite easy to wake up a sleeping person or animal – a light touch or even a sharp noise will do it.

In hibernation an animal's body behaves differently. Breathing is slowed down to a mere 'tick-over'; the circulation is also feeble; digestion ceases, and the animal cannot be roused by a touch or sound.

All reptiles are cold-blooded and when they hibernate they tend to do so deeply – more deeply than those warm-blooded creatures that hibernate. However, in both cold and warm-blooded animals fat is stored up during the warmer months, and it is on this that they rely for their survival throughout this resting period.

It puzzles some people as to why such animals or tortoises, which come from hot – even tropical – countries should require to hibernate. What is forgotten is that though the temperature during the day in such countries may be quite warm, at night, during the season that corresponds to our winter, the temperature may drop a great deal – quite enough for a human being to feel cold, and more than enough to affect a cold-blooded animal which, you will remember, depends so much on the temperature of its surroundings.

In the wild, tortoises usually dig themselves in some distance below the ground level and there they remain safe from cold until the warm season comes round again. It is the gradual warming up of the earth that starts to arouse the hibernating tortoises, and in nature they will not become really active until the nights as well as the days have a reasonable level of temperature.

With your pet tortoises you must allow them to behave as nearly as possible to what they would do in their native countries.

The most important thing is for you to realize that the months of activity and feeding are tied up with eventual preparation for hibernation – particularly after mid-summer. When a tortoise comes out after its winter rest it will have lost weight, and to begin with, weight must be regained by feeding up. Under decent weather conditions feeding will then continue all through the spring and summer; but towards the middle of August you must be sure that your tortoises are feeding well and regularly upon the most nourishing foodstuffs. Unless they are fully fed and feel heavy, they may not have put on enough fat to last them through the coming months. If this is the case they should not be hibernated but brought inside to a heated cage where they would remain awake and feed.

You may find that from mid-September onwards your tortoises may appear, all of a sudden, to be eating less. So long as they are in good health otherwise, you need not worry about this. The days may feel quite warm to you, but a tortoise is much more sensitive to changes of temperature than you are, and this slacking off of feeding is due to the cooler weather causing the tortoises' body functions, such as digestion and respiration, to slow down, until they refuse food altogether and no longer move about. Unless the *nights* as well as the days are unusually warm you should, by the beginning of October at the latest, be putting your tortoises away into their winter quarters.

About this time of year and also in the spring, there are times when the days are quite warm and the tortoises will feed, but the nights are too cold for them to be left outside. They should therefore be brought in at night in case there is any ground frost. The tortoise may not settle down and hibernate but remain awake. A large number of tortoise owners allow their pets to roam about at this time even though they are not feeding. This is harmful because the tortoise is using up its store of fat and is not replacing it. The rule is, if it is warm enough for the tortoise to feed, allow it to do so. If not, it should go into hibernation where it will have less opportunity of using up its stored fat even if it is too warm for it to sleep.

It used to be quite common for those who kept tortoises to let them just dig themselves into the earth in the garden when they felt like it; nowadays I think this careless way of dealing with them is less common – I certainly hope it is.

Letting a tortoise dig itself into the earth is very unwise for more than one reason. In the first place you must remember that in the countries where our tortoises come from the ground may be stony, but it is sandy in between the rocks and stones. It is soft, and therefore it is easy for a tortoise to dig down deep enough for complete protection.

In your gardens the soil may be gravelly, or clay, and even if it is sandy it will not be so easy to dig into as the sand in the normal habitat abroad. A tortoise will not realize this and will often dig only as far as it can do so easily. This will nearly always not be deep enough to protect it from frosts and it will then run a great risk of dying during the winter.

There is a further danger in allowing a tortoise to bury itself where it chooses – you will often not know it has done so, and therefore you will have no idea what spot it has selected. Apart from being very desirable to know where your pet has gone, there is another, much greater danger. The spot chosen will most likely be in a flower bed or vegetable patch where the earth is at least 'workable'. This is just the kind of place where someone will in due course dig when preparing the garden. Many a tortoise has been speared by accident with a garden fork. One of my earliest tortoise pets perished in this way, and this taught me, when I was quite a small boy, not to let a tortoise dig itself in for the winter in some unknown spot. In fact, I have never since allowed any of my tortoises to hibernate in this manner.

How, then, should you go about providing a tortoise with a winter resting place?

First think about what I have told you of a tortoise's normal habits and requirements. It likes the feeling of being 'buried'; although it must be cold to hibernate, it must have protection from frost and damp; and it must be in a place where the temperature does not vary to any great extent. This is because the only way in which a hibernating tortoise can be aroused is by warmth; and if the place where the tortoise is housed for the winter is subject to rises and falls of temperature now and then, this will have a very unsettling effect on its internal organs and may well cause death. The following is the proper way to go about hibernating your tortoise (or tortoises).

You must have a wooden box not less than 2 feet deep, although a larger one would be better. A tea chest which you may be able to obtain from a grocer quite cheaply will last for years. These tea chests are usually made with metal strips at the corners, and these go some way towards preventing rats or mice gnawing their way into the box and then finding the tortoise and proceeding to nibble at the shell which, you should remember, is a living substance. For the same reason you must cover the top of the box either with perforated zinc – which is the best material – or with small mesh wire netting folded back on itself so as to make the mesh too small for a mouse to get in – this is not easy to do, and I prefer the perforated zinc. Having got your box ready, make sure that the box is dry and then put in straw, hay, dry leaves, dry sphagnum moss or even shredded paper : all are good insulating material. Press down this bedding so that it feels firm.

Next put your tortoise, which must be in good condition, into a small well-ventilated cardboard box (somewhat larger than the tortoise), fill the box with some of the insulating material you are using, then tie it up. The

perforated zinc

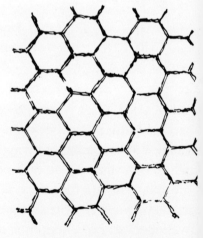

small mesh wire netting

small box containing the tortoise should then be placed into the larger box and covered over with the rest of the insulating material. Place the cover in position and tack it down firmly; put a blanket over your tea-chest or box.

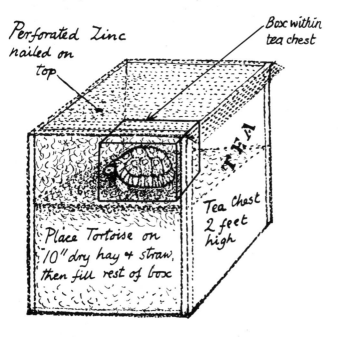

Perforated Zinc nailed on top

Box within tea chest

TEA

Tea Chest 2 feet high

Place Tortoise on 10" dry hay + straw, then fill rest of box

The actual place where you decide to leave your hibernation box for the winter period is very important indeed. The best kind of place is in an outhouse, garden shed, disused stable or even in a corner of an *unheated* garage.

Having put the box in position, on a bench off the ground, leave it quite *undisturbed*. Resist any temptation to have a look now and then to see if the tortoise is all right. If you have fed it well during the summer and it is in good trim, and the quarters you have provided are as I have set out, you should have no trouble.

Many tortoises have died when placed in a large hibernation box, through moving to the surface of the insulating material during a warm spell and being caught where they are more exposed when the colder weather returned. The tortoise will be woken by warm spells even if it is hibernating in a double box but it will soon settle down again if it is left alone. What you should not do is to take it out of hibernation and put it outside, because even if it is a sunny day it will not be warm enough for it to feed, and this will cause it to use up its stored fat far more quickly. Using the two box method of hibernating tortoises is also useful when there is more than one tortoise, as it prevents one tortoise from disturbing another.

So much for hibernation itself. But it is as important to know how to deal with your tortoise the following spring as it is to put it away for the cold season correctly.

AFTER HIBERNATION

Let us imagine that your tortoise has been left alone and untouched throughout late autumn and winter; the problem now is to decide when to have a look to see if all is well. You must use your common sense here: if the winter has been late and March finds your part of the country in the grip of hard frost or under a cover of snow, it is clear that your tortoise should remain where it is – in its box. If, on the other hand, there is an early spring and the temperature in mid-March is around 18·5° C

(60° F) (as it is in some years), and the weather forecasts predict that the thermometer will remain at that temperature for a few days, then you can uncover your hibernation box and inspect your tortoise.

It is highly probable under these weather conditions that the tortoise will show some signs of emerging from its hibernating state. Its eyes may be open and when you pick it up it may move its head and legs a little. This is a good sign and you can carry on with your inspection. First of all look at the shell to make sure it has not been damaged by mice or rats in spite of your precautions. If there are any signs of injury to the shell take it to a veterinary surgeon who will give you a quick-acting substance to ensure that no infection sets in and that the raw place will heal.

If all is well and no rodents have got into the box during the winter, you must then go in for the same examination as you did when you first bought your tortoise (see Chapter 4). See that the eyes will open and shut without difficulty; this you can easily test by placing a finger very gently over the eye and watching for the reaction of the eyelids. Should you find the eyelids closed, and that a sort of hard crust has formed round them, you should first try to loosen the crust and then remove it by bathing the eyes in warm water to which a *little* boracic powder has been added – even an eye lotion such as is used in your house may be successful, but add a little warm water to it to take off the chill. These measures will usually put matters right with the eyes and also with the nostrils and lips, which occasionally get stuck up too. If the crust is very difficult to get away try using a little warm olive oil. If you find much inflammation when you have removed it, do not try home treatment, but take the tortoise to a vet at once.

Let us hope, however, that your inspection has not disclosed anything alarming. You may now take the tortoise into the sun – we have already imagined a fine warm day. Put it on the lawn or in the pen, so long as the sun is shining there, and leave it alone while you get a basin half-filled with clean *warm* water. By the time you have done this the tortoise may have put out its head and legs – a further good sign. Place it in the basin but make sure that the water does not cover its head. Wait patiently to see what happens. As I said earlier on, there may be a small discharge of waste matter, but this should only be slight, since tortoises normally stop feeding *before* they go into hibernation and so have little food – if any – inside them which requires digestion. If there is any discharge then remove the tortoise and pour the soiled water down a drain; refill the basin as before and put the tortoise into it again. This immersion serves two purposes: it helps to warm up the tortoise and it gives an opportunity for drinking which is often the first thing the creature does on emergence from hibernation.

Do not worry if no food is taken during the first few days after the winter's rest has ended. Offer some tomato segments and fresh lettuce, or some of its favourite food, but do not be surprised if these are ignored. A tortoise

66

takes some little time to warm up so early in the year, but an hour or so out in the open on every sunny day will help gradually to make it more active. If the weather holds and the day temperature remains about 12·8° C – 15·5° C (55° F – 60° F) you may expect your pet to become more and more active and to start feeding again.

However, it is much too early yet for you to put your tortoise into its pen and leave it there. You must take it in after a few hours' basking and replace it in its hibernating box well before sundown. Unless the weather in April sets in very warm and dry you should not give a tortoise the freedom of its pen and shelter until May when, with any luck, frosts should be slight or even absent. Even then, it is advisable to put the tortoise into its shelter at night until it goes in voluntarily. You must study the weather and act accordingly – don't just go by the month of the year.

Most people who have trouble over hibernating their tortoises do not carry out the rules; if you do as I have described, you should not encounter any real difficulty.

9 Breeding

Up to about 1938 it was rare to hear accounts of pet tortoises laying eggs and, as far as I know, there were no reports of tortoises in this country actually mating and then eggs being produced. You may wonder what is the difference between a tortoise laying eggs in captivity, and *mating* and then laying eggs. The explanation is quite interesting.

To begin with, thirty or more years ago far fewer people kept tortoises than today, and those who did so mostly failed to observe them carefully. If eggs were discovered they were usually thrown away, possibly because there were not many sources of information to go to for advice. Today people take more interest in their pets and there are animal societies, lecturers and writers on pets, and more zoos where help and advice can be obtained. This means that more reports of egg-laying come to light.

As for the eggs themselves, these are most frequently produced by female tortoises that have mated *before* arriving in this country. It is a peculiarity of certain tortoises and terrapins that the females lay fertile eggs for a number of years, possibly three or four, after a single mating, though the number of fertile eggs in the clutch will be fewer each year. Consequently a female tortoise which has been bought from a pet-shop *may* later lay eggs without there being a male companion. And female tortoises can lay unfertile eggs, and often do. There have been instances of solitary females laying unfertile eggs even after twenty years of captivity.

In addition to the eggs which are produced in this way. there have been, in the last ten to fifteen years, reliable reports of tortoises actually mating and laying fertile eggs in this country – the eggs afterwards hatching successfully. These interesting cases have, of course, occurred when a true pair of tortoises have been kept and, most significant, they have occurred during the few really hot summers which we have had during that period.

These are the circumstances under which tortoise eggs may be laid in what must be, for them, a foreign and not very suitable climate. So I think I ought to give a brief account of the breeding habits of the tortoises which we keep as pets – an account of what happens under their natural conditions in their native lands.

Having mated, the female digs a hole in the soil. The digging is done mostly with the *hind* feet and the hole will be about four to five inches or so deep, according to the number of eggs to be laid. The number will depend upon the age of the female, and is anything from three to twelve, the smaller numbers indicating a young female. While this little pit is being excavated, the female may moisten the earth with water from her own body. The eggs are deposited in the 'nest' and the hole is carefully covered over in such a manner as to leave no obvious tell-tale traces which might attract the attention of an enemy.

In the wild it is difficult to say exactly how long incubation takes, but it is in the region of eight to ten weeks. The eggs themselves are white and roughly the size of a wood-pigeon's egg.

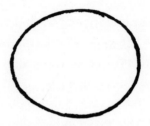

Egg of spur-thighed tortoise
(actual size)

When the young tortoises hatch, they push their way to the surface and under normal conditions will eat after about a day. The parent tortoise takes no notice of them for she departs from the nesting site as soon as she has laid her eggs, and they have to fend for themselves.

All this applies almost entirely to wild tortoises. Now let us think about the care of tortoise eggs which may be laid in this country; but I must make it clear that successful hatching out, though more frequent now than it used to be, is by no means certain.

The most common thing to happen is for the owner to look in his pen or enclosure one day and find some eggs casually laid among the earth and stones. This will be because egg-laying is not normally expected and few people arrange in their pens an area of sand deep enough for a tortoise to dig into. As soon as the eggs are found they should be marked on the upper side with a pencil and picked up carefully. Tortoise eggs should not be turned; otherwise they will spoil and this is the reason for marking the tops. They should then be placed in a tin or box. The box should be filled to within 2 inches from the top with fine sand – silver sand is best – with which is mixed a *little* sifted peat moss. This mixture could be very slightly damp but on no account *wet*. Eggs have also hatched in dry sand or on cotton wool.

The container must now be put in some place where the temperature will not drop below about 23.9° C (75° F), and not rise above 30° C (86° F). This is not easy in some households, but a good airing cupboard with a hot water tank in it can prove quite a successful incubator. If the airing cupboard cannot provide the correct temperature, the box should be placed in a small aquarium with a lamp in the lid. The temperature should be checked with a thermometer. The eggs will take less time to hatch at a higher temperature than at a lower one. After putting the box away, it must not be disturbed nor the eggs moved. After – say – ten weeks, it is wise to look into the box each day in case there are signs of hatching. This must be continued daily until twenty weeks in all have gone by; give it another week just in case, and if there are no baby tortoises appearing by then, your luck is out. In the past there have been cases of eggs hatching as long as twenty weeks after laying. This is unusual, however, as they usually hatch within 12–14 weeks. If the eggs are held up to a strong light, you will be able to see whether or not an embryo has started to develop. If there is no sign of an embryo you will know that the eggs were unfertile. The eggs can be examined when they are laid but I must emphasize once again that they must be handled very carefully and not turned.

If you have a pair of tortoises and you have reason to believe that they are in really good condition it may be worth while clearing a square yard or so in your enclosure. Rake away the stones and dig the earth thoroughly, passing it through a sieve to remove any other stones. Having done this, remove about three-quarters of the loose earth and replace it with some fine sand; mix the earth and sand together and level off the surface. This may possibly be used by your female tortoise, if she mates successfully, as a suitable place for digging her nest-hole. As I have already explained, you will be unlikely to have mating and the laying of fertile eggs unless the summer is exceptionally warm for long periods.

You can judge fairly well whether your tortoises will mate by watching their courtship behaviour – yes, tortoises do indeed indulge in courtship. It is a rough affair and rather comical: the male tortoise will be observed butting the female time and time again. He will go as near as a tortoise can to taking a run at the rear end of her shell, ending up with quite a thump. This can go on for some while, and may be renewed on subsequent days. If the weather is fair and you have noted the courtship be-

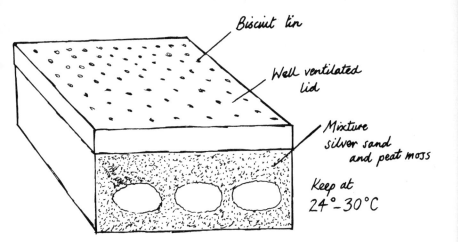

Improvised 'incubator'

haviour you may be lucky enough to see the eventual digging out of the 'nest' and even to watch the eggs being laid, but you must be most careful not to frighten the female by sudden sounds or movements. However, it is more likely that the egg-laying will be carried out when you are not there; but if you examine, very keenly, the area you prepared for the egg-laying, you may be able to spot very faint signs of disturbance on the surface of the sandy soil, which will be a clue to what has happened.

You will now be faced with a problem. Shall you leave things to luck and take a chance on the weather, or not? I can only give my personal opinion on this point. As we seldom get two really hot summers in succession, I should be reluctant to take the risk of leaving the eggs where they were laid in case they did not hatch or were discovered by a magpie or crow, which would make a good meal of them. I think, then, you will have greater chances of success if you go through the same process as I described in the cases when the eggs are laid haphazard by a single female.

Remember that the chances against hatching the eggs are heavy in either case; but if you go in for artificial incubation, you will at least have no fear of enemies, and the temperature side will be more or less under control. Try your best and hope for the best, but do not be too disappointed if you fail – you may always have another opportunity the next summer.

We must now consider what you should do if you are successful and you find yourself the proud foster-parent of, perhaps, half a dozen or so baby tortoises, newly hatched and about the size of a large walnut.

You will, of course, want to know where to keep these and how to look after them; but I must warn you that if you do have the luck to hatch out several of them, you must not be too disappointed if one or two die. This is because when a number of baby tortoises are hatched, some may be weaker than others.

First put them in a box lined with newspaper or, better still, an old aquarium tank with newspaper folded so as to cover the bottom – this helps to keep them warm. Warmth is important at this stage, for if the youngsters get chilled they will die.

You must change the newspaper every day and must watch carefully, once the babies start to feed, to see that they are producing droppings regularly.

The tank or box should be kept *indoors* and preferably in a room which is normally the warmest in the house – in any case the temperature around the tank should never fall below 20° C (68° F). This means that unless you live in a very cold house where, perhaps, the central heating is left on in one or two of the rooms, you will have to supply some form of artificial heating. The easiest way to do this is to have a tin box, with the lid *off*, which is sufficiently large to have your tank or box resting on top of it. A hole should be made in one side of the box, about the middle, and into this should be fixed an electric lamp bulb-holder with the flex run to some convenient lighting point. A bulb of 25 watts should be sufficient to keep the tank warm enough during the time when the sun is not shining.

However, this is not enough for dull days, for we must remember that sunlight is as necessary for newly hatched tortoises as it is for adults. When sunlight falls on a window-sill – which is a suitable place for your tank to be put – you must be able to move the tank so that the baby tortoises can enjoy direct sunlight for as long as possible. You must be careful if the tortoises are housed in a poorly ventilated aquarium as these become overheated when placed in front of a sunlit window. It would be preferable to place them in a shallow wooden box while sunning them in front of the window. However, it is possible that you may have the bad luck not to be able to arrange for the tank to receive sunlight at all. If this is so, and the tortoises are housed in an aquarium with a lid, a light should be fitted inside. If you do not have this type of accommodation, you can use an adjustable reading lamp so placed that it will shine directly down on the tortoises. The lamp should be about 12 inches above the tank and a 60-watt bulb will usually be sufficient. Let me remind you that the light is a source of warmth for the baby tortoises as they can bask under it as they would the sun, but they will not receive any health-giving rays as they would if exposed to direct sunlight. A small shelter would allow them to escape from the light when they wish to sleep.

You will have to use your common sense in connexion with the actual placing of the tank, and it must not be so situated that it is in a draught.

The only alternative to this is to give your baby tortoises to a zoo or to some other person who can provide the conditions required.

I must warn you that when the babies first hatch out their shells will be on the soft side, so handle them very gently indeed – this softness will pass off soon after feeding begins, so long as you give the right food. You may

Newly hatched
tortoise
(actual size)

find that the newly hatched tortoises will not feed at all for a day or two. Do not worry about this, for they will still be getting nourishment from what remains of the yolk of the egg in which they were enclosed.

Now for feeding. Baby tortoises will eat most of the foods that are taken by adults provided it is finely chopped or shredded; they cannot do much in the way of tackling whole leaves and so on. Offer them shredded lettuce or small clover leaves, and also thin slices of tomato. Do not forget a little tinned dog or cat food. You must give, in addition, a pinch of mineral mixture supplement or bone meal, or even *powdered* cuttle-fish-bone. This you can provide easily by scraping the soft side of the 'bone' and then crushing this further with the back of a spoon. Scatter your pinch of the powder over the lettuce and tomato. This will help with shell growth and must be continued throughout their lives. As to how much food to give, I can only say that you should offer food at least twice a day and be guided by the amount the babies eat. Never leave any food to get stale; throw away the uneaten food after about an hour or so and replace it each time with fresh.

Tortoises grow very slowly and you must not attempt to hibernate babies; you will have to keep up your feeding all through the first winter and probably the second winter as well. When spring comes along you can put out your youngsters on a lawn or in a yard on sunny days, but they must be put back into their tank or box each night. Do *not* put them outside on dull or damp days, and

77

when they are indoors they must be protected from draughts.

What about drinking? At first I would suggest you offer each tortoise separately a little tepid water from a tiny saucer or lid of a tin. You must hold the tortoise in one hand and gently bring its nose nearer the water until it touches it. If you cannot get the baby tortoises to drink, sprinkle a little water over their food. This will ensure they receive some water. I would advise you to leave a shallow dish of water, no more than ½ inch deep, in their tank as they may be attracted by the smell of water and might enter for a bath. It would do no harm to place them in their baths if they do not go in voluntarily, as long as the temperature of the water is about 26·7° C (80° F). Their tank should be about the same temperature, and you should ensure that there is no possibility of their being in a draught.

I expect you may think that all the instructions I have given you seem like hard work – and so it is; but if you are not prepared to do what is necessary you should not keep a tortoise at all, let alone try to rear baby ones. If you do succeed in rearing babies you will have great satisfaction and pleasure as the results of your care and attention.

10 Terrapins

Before discussing the requirements of terrapins in captivity, there are a few observations I would like to make first. It is most important that you realise that buying a terrapin or any other animal is a very serious matter, and unless you are prepared to give the time and to accept the responsibility involved you should not own one. Many thousands are imported into this country every year but very few survive; the majority are subjected to a cruel existence and a lingering death. This is because few people have any idea of a terrapin's requirements. Quite often customers are misinformed at the time of purchase. Some terrapins are received as gifts by people who have little interest in them. They are also purchased on impulse by irresponsible people who soon tire of them. If only advice were sought first, there would be fewer deaths, because if kept in proper conditions and on a correct diet they will live for many years.

There are approximately 60 species of terrapins imported into the country, the majority of which are rarely seen in the local pet shop and are usually imported by dealers who specialize in reptiles and are sold to professional and amateur herpetologists. The remaining species are the ones that are imported in their thousands and are sold in the local pet shops. Two species come from Europe and North Africa. The European Pond Tortoise, *Emys orbicularis*, which is either black or grey with yellow spots on the head and neck and radiating yellow lines on the shields of the black shell. The second is the Spanish terrapin, *Clemmys caspica leprosa*, which has a greyish brown shell and yellow lines on a grey neck. A third terrapin comes from South America; this is the Ornate Terrapin, *Pseudemys ornate callirostris*. Its softer parts have a green background; there are faint red markings behind the eyes and yellow spots on the mouth and chin, and circular markings on the green shell. The last species originates from North America; this is the 'Red Eared' terrapin, *Pseudemys scripta elegans*, which has a bright green shell. The head and neck is also green with thin yellow lines, with two prominent red marks behind the eyes.

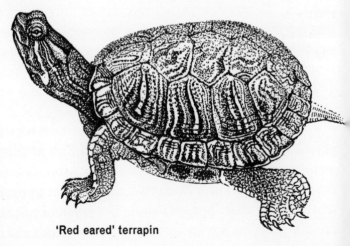

'Red eared' terrapin

European pond tortoise

Before buying a terrapin some thought should have been given to the facilities you can offer. Possibly you have a natural pond where the hardier European species could live outside summer and winter. Alternatively, you may be restricted to an aquarium. That being so, it would be as well to remember that some terrapins may grow to 10 inches and would require a tank of approximately 36 inches in length.

It is the hatching 'Red Eared' and Ornate terrapins that come over in their thousands and are sold as miniatures by some dealers who should know better. I strongly advise against buying them at this size as the majority of them rarely survive. These baby terrapins arrive when only a few weeks old and there are a number of factors hindering their chances of survival. Among them are the conditions they are kept in after hatching. If they are kept in vast numbers in small containers quite a number will get little opportunity of feeding. Also mortality will be high in the event of an epidemic. Then there is the

Ornate terrapin

journey, the way they are packed and the temperature during transit.

When you are in the shop, have a look at the way they are being housed. The Ornate and 'Red Eared' terrapins should be kept at a temperature of approximately 26·7° C (80° F), so unless the shop is exceptionally warm, which I doubt, they should be in heated tanks with a lamp above them. Check what food they have been offered and whether it is fresh. (See the section on feeding.) If all they have had is a proprietary brand of dried turtle food, do not buy your terrapins here, as this is an inadequate diet. Is the water fresh? Naturally it will look dirty if they are feeding, but if it has not been changed for some days the scum will be noticeable. Reject any with swollen or inflamed lids; they should have clear, bright eyes. Reject also those with fungus and injuries or those that list to one side when swimming. Do not buy any if there are parasitic worms in the tank. I would not purchase any with carapaces (shells) less than 2 to 3 inches; at this size their shells should be hard if they are healthy. Finally, do not buy these plastic turtle bowls as they are not large enough to provide suitable conditions for maintaining young terrapins in good health.

HOUSING OUT OF DOORS

Under suitable conditions European species could live out of doors throughout the year. The most important factor is: can they hibernate safely during the winter months? In the wild, as the colder weather approaches, they will bury themselves some 12 inches or more in the mud at the bottom of the pond or stream, or, if the earth is soft enough, into the mud on the banks. If you are wondering how terrapins can spend the winter asleep under water and without air, you will remember when we were talking about hibernation of tortoises, we said that the functions of the body are almost at a standstill and this includes breathing. Also some terrapins are able to absorb oxygen from the water, and the little that is required during natural hibernation would be sufficient for their needs. If then you have a natural pond or a large ornamental pool containing about 12 inches of mud, they should hibernate safely during the winter. I must warn you, however, that unless the garden is escape proof, you will require an effective barrier to confine them, as terrapins are able to burrow and climb obstacles far more successfully than tortoises.

If you are considering building an ornamental pond

for terrapins there are a number of factors to be taken into account before you start:

(1) A few terrapins could live in a large pool that would not require draining as the aquatic life in the pond would clear any scraps left by the terrapins. As a guide, I am thinking of no more than 6 terrapins in a pool with a surface area of 5 feet × 10 feet. If it is deep enough for you to have about 12 inches of mud on the bottom, they would safely hibernate there during the winter. If this is not possible, they will have to be removed and hibernated elsewhere (hibernation will be discussed later).

(2) If you wish to keep large numbers of terrapins, the water will need changing after every meal, and the pool will require draining.

(3) The pool could have steep sides to prevent the terrapins from climbing out, providing an island is built in the centre for the terrapins to climb on to.

(4) If there is not an island there must be an area round the pool or at one end where the terrapins can climb out.

In the smaller ponds that require frequent changes of water, it may be difficult to provide aquatic plants for the terrapins to hide beneath; therefore two pieces of rock with a third laid across them would form an underwater retreat. Access to the dry area should be facilitated by a gentle slope. If you do not have the facilities for building a pool you might consider buying a fibre-glass one. You will, of course, have to make provision for draining and cleaning, either by placing the pool on a raised bank which would permit the use of a hose pipe from the bottom of the pool to a drain. Alternatively, you could use a small pump which would be concealed among some rock and could also provide a small waterfall which would add to the attraction of the pool.

A few words now about the area surrounding the pool. Basically this would be the same as for tortoises. There should, however, be a little more shrubbery, tufts of grass and other plants, and the open areas should contain more soil with a mixture of soil and sand in places, as terrapins like to bury themselves. There should be one or two flat stones on which they can bask. A small cave filled with sphagnum moss could be built with a few pieces of rock. Some terrapins will avail themselves of this shelter, though the majority of them take to the water on cooler days. Remember terrapins, like tortoises, require the warmth of the sun if they are to function properly. Tropical specimens should be given the opportunity of going outside on warm days during the summer months, but when the temperature drops and they stop feeding they should be brought inside. European specimens should be brought in about late September or early October, depending on the temperature, if they are not hibernating outside.

HIBERNATION

The European Pond tortoise and the Spanish terrapin may be hibernated in very similar conditions to tortoises. In fact, I know of a number of cases where these specimens have been hibernated in the exact conditions

Spanish terrapin

mentioned in the chapter on hibernation. The usual procedure, however, is to fill a very large box with loose damp earth mixed with leaves or moss. Some terrapins will dig down themselves, others will have to be buried. The box should be kept in a garage or unheated shed. They will wake as the weather becomes warmer in the spring. This may be in March or April. One cannot give a date because this does depend on the temperature. They may then be returned to their outside pond. If there is a chance of frost, however, they should be brought in at night.

HOUSING INDOORS

Terrapins can be kept in the simplest of containers for many years provided proper attention is given to their diet, habits, heating and lighting requirements.

The ideal home for small terrapins is an aquarium. It may be set up in the following manner. Two pieces of rock placed on the bottom of the tank should support a third piece forming a platform. The underside of the platform should be about 1 inch above the surface of the water; this allows the terrapin to surface for air whilst in its retreat. The security these underwater retreats offer to the more nervous specimens is often essential to their well-being. To aid the terrapin in leaving the water, a fourth piece of rock should be suitably placed against one of the supports so that it forms a shelving ramp. A dry retreat should be provided on the platform; this could be made from a broken flower pot or a piece of curved bark.

Very young terrapins will require about an inch or so of water until they acclimatize; larger ones will naturally require more. I do not recommend gravel or water plants as they will make the daily changing of water, which is a simple process, a very troublesome one. However, there is no need for the tank to be unsightly; with a little imagination they can be quite decorative. Instead of having the usual 24″ × 12″ tank, why not a 24″ × 15″ × 12″ or even 24″ × 18″ × 12″. The extra height will allow you to suspend two or three small potted plants such as Tradescantia, Philodendron or Ficus Primula. There are a number of little plastic or wire flower pot baskets on the market. The plants will hang down above the water but out of reach of the terrapins. You could, of course, construct a more elaborate vivarium providing conditions that would encourage terrapins to breed. The vivarium in the illustration on page 89 has a 36 inch aquarium, with a drain, for the terrapins to swim in. The dry area consists of a mixture of sand and soil, with some rock and a few plants in a fibre-glass box. The sides and top are of perspex, gauze and glass, and the base is boxed in with wood. Instead of an aquarium you could use a small fibre-glass pool and have the dry area either side of the pool. Whatever the size or the design, there are a number of basic points to remember. Provision must be made for drainage not only from the pool, but also the bank, as the plants will require spraying every now and again. The water may be removed by buckets or if it can be arranged, direct by hose pipe. Use only three or four pieces of rock in the pool for access and shelter. Proper attention must be given to ventilation, heating and lighting. Some rock placed underneath a lamp would make an excellent basking site and would also afford some shade if there was provision for the terrapin shelter beneath it.

HEATING AND LIGHTING

Tropical terrapins, and I am including the young 'Red Eared', require a temperature between 24·4° C (76° F) to 29° C (85° F), during the day, depending on individual preference, if they are to feed and digest their food properly. The temperature may be allowed to drop a few degrees at night. To maintain this temperature, you will have to buy a small heater and thermostat. These are not very expensive and are the same as those used in tropical fish aquaria. For smaller tanks containing only a few inches of water, you will be able to purchase a heater with a lower wattage. Unlike fish aquaria, however, our

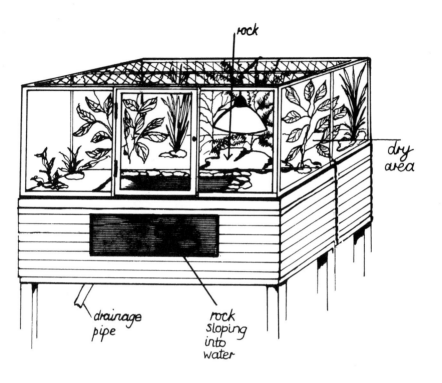

rock

dry area

drainage pipe

rock sloping into water

heaters are not covered by gravel and will need protecting from the terrapins. Indeed, even if they were covered, the terrapins would soon uncover them. The safest method I have found is to house them in a 'cage' of perforated zinc. A section of the zinc is cut out, a little larger than the heater, and rolled into a cylinder. The heater is fixed inside and is thus protected from the attentions of the terrapins. It may be placed out of sight behind the rock. A lamp should be fitted above the rock allowing them to bask. The temperature should not rise much above 30° C (86° F) at the basking area. Although they will not receive the same benefit from the lamp as they would from the sun, the lamp is important as it gives them opportunity to behave as they would in the wild by coming out of the water, lying under the lamp and returning to the water when they have absorbed enough heat.

European terrapins being housed indoors would be content with a lamp for basking during the summer months, but they would require a proper heater and thermostat during the winter if they are not being put into hibernation.

FEEDING

Under natural conditions, terrapins feed daily on a great variety of animal life as well as plants. The following list will give you some idea. Frogs and newts and their larvae, fish, snails, freshwater shrimps and other crustaceans, spiders, insects, earthworms; in fact, most of the aquatic invertebrates that are large enough to make a meal. They will also feed on members of other vertebrates such as small snakes, lizards, other terrapins and even small dead birds and mammals if they happen to come across any. You can now understand why if some dealers tell you that terrapins will thrive on these packets of dried turtle food, it is likely the terrapins in their shops are undernourished. Also, it is no wonder so many thousands of them die every year after a long period of suffering in captivity. They should be fed as much of their natural food as you are able to provide. If you live in town, it will be impossible to offer enough of their natural food each day; indeed, during some parts of the year you would be unable to provide any of it. Here is another list of food to keep them healthy: fish, particularly raw herring or sprats, which are exceptionally nourishing, shrimps, liver, raw steak, kidney, hearts, watercress, lettuce, fruit and white bread. Do not forget to offer any insects or earthworms you manage to find. The food should be placed in the water, although in time your terrapin will learn to take food from your fingers.

Terrapins, especially the babies, are healthier on daily feeds but it does not do any great harm if they miss an occasional meal. Terrapins need plenty of calcium especially while they are young, which is why they should be fed the whole fish. The baby terrapins will be able to manage small pieces of sprat, so try to include some bone as well as the entrails and flesh. You might be able to get a few young snails from your pet shop and this will give them some extra calcium. Small earthworms will contain a number of minerals and your baby terrapins could certainly manage one if it was chopped before offering it.

Remember that terrapins are mainly carnivorous but do require a little vegetation. Indeed, certain species seem to increase the amount of vegetable matter they eat as they get older. If you are worried about the calcium intake in an otherwise healthy terrapin, cut up a few pieces of meat that are small enough to be swallowed without having to be torn up and dip one side of them in some bone meal, calcium powder or mineral mixture, then fold it over so that the mineral content is inside; when offered to the terrapin it should be swallowed before it tastes the powder.

CLEANING

The tank should be thoroughly cleaned out and the rock scrubbed after every meal, and refilled with water of the correct temperature. This is why I advise keeping the lay-out of the tank simple; it is then only a few minutes' work. Remember to wash your hands after cleaning out the tank. You should of course wash whenever you have handled an animal. It is also advisable to pour a drip of disinfectant down the drain.

Some people feed their terrapins in a second bowl or tank containing water of the correct temperature. When they are thought to have finished feeding, their shells are wiped clean and then they are returned to their tanks.

But who is to know when they have enough to eat? I certainly don't. Most terrapins will return to a meal any number of times during the day. The usual reason for this practice is that owners wish to have an attractive lay-out in the terrapin tank which they do not want to get dirty or to disturb because of the work it involves. I feel some terrapins are going to suffer because of this practice. I said, earlier, that if we wish to keep these exotic animals in captivity, then their health and requirements must come first. Also, I have heard of cases where people will not feed herring to their terrapins because of the mess it makes. They go on to say that terrapins do not feed on herrings in the wild and their argument sounds reasonable at first, but remember, in captivity, they are going without most of their natural food and also, very important, sunlight. These have got to be made up in other ways.

BREEDING

Under ideal conditions terrapins will breed in captivity. They become sexually mature at 5–7 years. Also, as with tortoises, a female may arrive with fertile eggs inside her and it is possible for females to lay fertile eggs at least three years after mating. If eggs are found out of the water, they should be treated exactly the same as tortoise eggs, with the exception of the medium they are buried in. In the case of terrapins, this should be kept a little on the damp side. They have been hatched in a mixture of sand, fine shingle and sphagnum moss. They have also been hatched on damp sterile wadding. The eggs should be kept at a temperature of 29° C (85° F), although a little lower or higher will not matter and will only lengthen or shorten the incubation period which is normally 3–5 months under artificial conditions. It is difficult to sex baby terrapins but before long the sexes are soon apparent. Male terrapins have long tails which are rather thick at the base. When viewed from below, the cloaca or vent is some distance from the shell. Certain males of the *Pseudemys* group, which includes the 'Red Eared' terrapin, have very long claws which they vibrate in the females' face during their courtship. Female terrapins have very short tails and when viewed from beneath, the cloaca is seen to be quite close to the shell.

11 Hints on Health

This chapter may surprise you because it is so short, but read it carefully all the same. The reason for its shortness is that I do not believe in home treatment for most of the ills that tortoises and terrapins suffer from – the right thing to do is to consult a veterinary surgeon. Many of them die because wrong treatment has been given.

There are far more tortoises, terrapins, and other reptiles being kept as pets today than in the past, and veterinary surgeons are becoming used to them as patients. Reptiles generally suffer from the same complaints as other animals, and modern drugs, antibiotics and other veterinary treatments are used successfully in reptiles. Various penicillin preparations act well on wounds, etc. Worm tablets that are used on mammals work equally well in reptiles, so also do certain antibiotics in combating various types of bacteria that get out of hand when your tortoise or terrapin is being kept incorrectly. The most important factor in any treatment is recognizing the symptoms early enough and this, I am afraid, is where we usually fail. Owing to their physical make-up reptiles can be feeding and to all intents and purposes appear quite well, when for no apparent reason they suddenly die. The post-mortem examination may show such severe internal disorders that, had the patient been a mammal or bird, it would have died weeks or even months earlier. This is why it is so important to keep your tortoises and terrapins correctly, offering a good diet and paying proper attention to their needs in regard to temperature, lighting and accommodation. The following paragraphs will give you an idea of the various ailments that tortoises and terrapins are liable to suffer from and a few hints on what action you should take.

Shell trouble. You may have trouble with a newly-bought tortoise which has small cracks in its shell, particularly on the underside. If these are not large and show no signs of infection you should have little cause for worry. However, if there is bleeding or other signs of injury, consult your veterinary surgeon. It is a normal occurrence in some terrapins and even occasionally in tortoises for whole shields to flake off due to growth. In the majority of species, however, the surface of the shields is gradually worn away while new growth is forming below. Soft shell is due to an incorrect diet, with a lack of calcium – I have already told you how to deal with this problem.

Cuts or other skin wounds. If the soft parts of a tortoise or terrapin get injured, first aid can be given by bathing the wound with warm water to remove any dirt; dab the place dry with a clean cloth and apply a disinfectant. Consult a veterinary surgeon as soon as you can. He will be able to treat the wound properly and advise you on how to continue the necessary measures.

Insect attacks. Tortoises may sometimes have the eggs of

blow-flies laid on their skin if this is soiled – especially if the dirt has collected round the tail. Unless the eggs are noticed quickly they will hatch into maggots which will feed on the flesh of your tortoise. If you have found eggs, wash the dirt and the eggs off with warm water, and dry. Should the eggs have hatched and the maggots be feeding, remove any you can by gentle bathing and seek expert advice at once. You can help to prevent this kind of thing happening by keeping your pen clean and removing any droppings daily – they attract the flies.

Worms. Tortoises and terrapins, like dogs and cats, can be troubled with worms. These may be seen in the droppings. Do not try any kind of treatment yourself, but put a few specimens into a clean jar or polythene bag and take them along to a vet. It is rather important that the vet sees the worms because there are different treatments required for the various worms.

Colds. Occasionally they may suffer from colds; the best treatment you can offer is to keep them warm and absolutely free from draughts. Your vet can supply antibiotics for serious cases. They may suffer a bout of constipation; in this case, try putting extra oil on their food. This may be rather difficult as most tortoises do not enjoy the taste of oil. I have, however, managed to get them to take halibut oil capsules placed inside a piece of their favourite food. Warm baths 29° C (85° F) will also help to relieve constipation.

Eyes. Terrapins often suffer from eye complaints shown to be due in most cases to an incorrect diet. The trouble is that once both eyes become affected and the animal is blind, it will not feed, so making it difficult to effect a cure. The terrapin gradually becomes weaker and dies. A large number of eye ailments, however, can be cured with one or other of the proprietary eye drops on sale in chemists.

Fungus. Another condition affecting terrapins is fungus, which must not be confused with the green algae that grows on the shells. Nor must it be confused with skin shedding, which is going on most of the time; this appears as very thin colourless strips floating almost free in the water with just one end attached to the neck or limbs. This also is normal. Fungus is of a thicker appearance, more like cotton wool; as often as not, there will be a small open wound or sore. If it is attacking the feet, claws are liable to drop out. Common salt sometimes helps, as does gentian violet. Some people have had some success with preparations that are sold to treat fungus in fish.

Occasionally some tortoises and terrapins just will not eat and for no apparent reason. One can only try opening their mouths, very gently, and placing small pieces of food inside. This is a difficult process but is well worth trying as it is sometimes successful.

A tip concerning terrapins. If they stop feeding suddenly and for no apparent reason, check the temperature; it may be that the heater is not functioning.

A point worth remembering – if your sick tortoise or terrapin is being housed in a heated room, do not just put it into a bag and take it out into the cold when visiting the vet. Put a hot water bottle in, taking care to keep the animal and bottle separate.

With proper housing, feeding, hibernation and, of course, good luck with the weather, your tortoise pets should not normally become invalids. Good food and warmth are the main requirements; and so long as you do your best to get a healthy tortoise or terrapin in the first place, you should not have to worry unduly about its well-being.

European pond tortoise

12 Some Observations on General Behaviour

Most people who keep any kind of pet are interested in its behaviour. They ought to be, since it is sometimes the case that even a novice will notice some activity or peculiarity which has not been observed before. Should this be so, notes should be taken in case, later on, what has been seen can be added to our general knowledge.

One normal piece of behaviour which any newcomer to tortoise-keeping should be able to observe is the way that your pets, when first placed in their enclosure, will explore the ground thoroughly. They will seem not only to be exploring, but also to be trying to find a way of escape. In my opinion, this is just what they are doing. Such behaviour does *not* mean that the creatures are 'unhappy'; this kind of activity occurs in many other animals when in captivity. It seems to be a natural instinct to examine, by one sense or another, the limit of the space in which they are confined.

On sunny days you will notice that when your land tortoises come out from their sleeping box they will find a place where the sun is shining strongly and here they will stay to 'warm up'. While doing this they will turn round once or twice so that all parts of their shells receive the heat necessary to make them active and ready to feed. As the day goes on they will alternate between feeding and resting; and if it is really hot they will go to a shady spot from time to time. When the evening comes and the sun is less strong, they will again seek out a warm place and also have a last feed before going back into their sleeping quarters.

Even a newly-acquired tortoise will not take many days to find its way to the shelter, and this power of 'location' is very interesting. Tortoises, when at liberty for a time in a garden, will soon find out, by sight and by scent, where certain plants are on which they like to feed. And so long as the plants concerned are there to find they will endeavour to go straight to them if allowed. I am of the opinion that tortoises have quite good memories for this kind of thing – quite apart from their eyesight and sense of smell. I have many times known a tortoise of mine find out, for instance, where garden peas are growing, or perhaps a bed of pansies. These will be visited regularly and attempts will be made to eat them. Try how you may, you will find it difficult – if not impossible – to prevent this. You can pick up a tortoise and take it away from the forbidden vegetable or flower and put it down in quite a different part of your garden; yet you will see that it will go as quickly and as straight as it can to the original spot time and time again.

Even more remarkable is the fact that I have known some of my tortoises 'remember' from year to year where certain delicacies have been previously found. They have come out of hibernation, and once they have started feeding regularly they have, when given an hour or two at liberty in the garden (under supervision!), made off at once in the direction of the place where peas or pansies have been. Of course these plants will not necessarily be growing there yet, or they may have been moved; but this does not seem to matter. Away the tortoises walk towards the original spot, and if tortoises can be said to look bewildered, then that is what they seem to be, for they will walk around seeking what is no longer there.

This seems to me to argue that though tortoises can locate food both by sight and by scent, they also have some lasting memory – perhaps a kind of picture – of where a particular food-stuff has been; and, moreover, they can find their way to the place unaided by vision or smell. This is something we do not yet understand about many animals – their precise methods of finding their way where ordinary senses would not seem to help them.

In spite of this seeming ability to navigate and to remember locations, it is true that both land tortoises and aquatic species are well known for 'straying' and subsequently getting lost. Over the years I have known many cases of this sort of behaviour. Only a year or two ago I had, in the course of one summer, a land tortoise and a Spanish Terrapin brought to me at separate times. In each instance the wanderer had been found at large, and though I made all possible inquiries in the neighbourhood, I was never able to trace the owners.

What happens is that a garden gate or door is left open when these pets are loose and unguarded, and they go off to explore. They are possibly unnoticed for some days and, once they go outside the area which they have known so well, they have no means of finding their way home again from any distance. The moral of this is – don't leave your pets free to roam unsupervised; and keep all gates and doors which enclose your premises shut.

I have already referred briefly to the senses of tortoises, but a little more about these may be of interest. It is difficult to say which of the senses is the most powerful in tortoises as a whole, because whereas we can to some extent test their ability to see and to recognize colours, it is not so easy to test their undoubtedly good sense of smell. I am inclined to think that their eyesight and powers of scent are about equal.

Many flowers are attractive to land tortoises – dandelions among the wild plants and pansies among garden plants would seem to be favourites. Pansies are usually mauve of some shade, or yellow; and although tortoises will, if they get the chance, feed on both, it is a fact that yellow ones are taken first if there is any choice. This is probably because tortoises perceive yellows more readily than mauves or blues. In this they seem to resemble sparrows, which so greedily go for crocuses and polyanthus flowers – the yellow ones appearing to be more attractive.

Reds seem to be less easily seen, though I have known this colour in flowers to be noticed and the blooms eaten. Whitish objects are soon spotted and many tortoises will go directly to a piece of banana if it is put down among other foods. However, this may be evidence of selection by scent, and the same probably applies to the readiness to eat tomato when it is offered.

Scent, then, is clearly of importance and it is interesting that I have never known a tortoise to nibble any kind of food and then reject it. This seems to show that food items are first tested with the nose and then accepted.

While I am sure that water tortoises and terrapins can smell well both in water and when on land, it is upon sight that they rely most. Remember that they depend mainly on live food, and therefore it is movement that attracts their attention. Just watch one of the aquatic species spot an earthworm in the water and you will have no doubt about their keen sense of sight. To what extent colours are of importance to them it is difficult to say, but there is no reason to doubt that they can distinguish certain colours. But movement is the principal stimulus in perceiving food as it is with frogs, toads, and lizards.

All kinds of tortoises and terrapins have a good sense of touch as can easily be demonstrated by placing a finger lightly on the head, legs or even tail; while a tap on the shell will make even a tame specimen withdraw quickly.

One last point. It is always preferable to keep two tortoises or terrapins rather than one, and if they are a pair they may possibly breed. This would be of great interest and no small achievement.

Index